PICTURE PARABLES

Children's Gospel Talks
for the OHP

by

Ceri Lusk

Illustrations by Rebecca Johnson

MOORLEY'S Print & Publishing

© Copyright 1998

All rights reserved. No part of this publication, except the illustrations,
may be reproduced, stored in a retrieval system, or
transmitted, in any form or by any means,
electronic, mechanical, photocopying, recording
or otherwise, without the prior
written permission of the publishers.

The drawings may only be copied
for the purpose of illustrating the
talks they accompany.

British Library Cataloguing in Publication Data.
A catalogue record for this book is available
from the British Library.

ISBN 0 86071 499 3

MOORLEY'S Print & Publishing
23 Park Rd., Ilkeston, Derbys DE7 5DA
Tel/Fax: (0115) 932 0643

Preface

The following selection of children's Gospel Talks have been given in holiday Bible Clubs as well as regular children's mid-week meetings. The targeted age-group has been mainly four to eight-year-olds although older children have sometimes been present.

Children's evangelism is always a challenging work and the following selection has been written and compiled in an effort to create a fresh approach to well known Bible truths.

The accompanying illustrations can be photocopied onto acetates, made into worksheets or simply copied.

Contents

1. **What are we really like?** 5
   (New hearts for old!)

2. **The Race** 18
   (Sin and a Saviour)

3. **Tommy Terror and Gordon Goodtoall** 29
   (The substitutionary death of Christ)

4. **Timmy and Tommy Trouble** 37
   (The substitutionary death of Christ)

5. **Sammy's Special Day** 48
   (The Good Shepherd)

6. **Freddy Fantastic's Fireworks Factory** 58
   (A Talk for Bonfire Night - Sin and a Saviour)

7. **Suzy's Christmas** 67
   (A seasonal Story)

8. **The Prince and the Teenie Weenies** 74
   (A Christmas Story)

9. **Noah's Flood** 88
   (Judgement and a Saviour)

10. **Ivor Nopennies and the Hidden Treasure** 96
    (Finding the true treasure)

What are we really like?
(New hearts for old)

What do we do if we want to check how we look? Do we just ask for another person's opinion? Usually we look in a mirror before we go out to check that our hair isn't sticking up all over the place. Did you know that the Bible is like a mirror? It tells us what we are really like but on the inside - that's different. Only God knows what we are like when we are on our own or out of the earshot of our mums and dads! God knows every thought we have, even before we think them. Sometimes we don't have very nice thoughts about others - God sees these too.

Well, we are going to take a look into someone's heart - I wonder what we will find!

Acetate 1 - 3

Perhaps we will find a Mitch Mean, a Grant Greedy or a Nigel Nosey? Mitch Mean never shares his sweets with anyone or if he does he makes sure he only offers the ones he dislikes! Grant Greedy always takes the last cake before waiting to find out if anyone else is interested. Nigel Nosey spends all his time putting that long nose in places he shouldn't. I wonder if we have any Scrooges, Greedy Pigs or Nosey Parkers here today? You just never know!

Acetate 4 & 5

Suddenly, Mitch Mean, Grant Greedy and Nigel Nosey jump out of their skins as a gruff voice shouts "Go away and leave me in peace." Ooh what an old Gavin Grump! His friend Bart Busy hurries off saying very quickly, "Oh I'm too busy to leave you in peace." Are you ever grumpy or too busy for others?

Acetate 6 - 8

"Go and get my slippers! Hurry up! Get me a drink while you're on your feet..." The voice carries on with one order after the next - not a please or a thank you in sight! What a bossy Boots! Naomi Naughty gets Beatrice Bossy a drink but tips it on the carpet just as she is about to give it to her. What a naughty miss. Fiona Fickle pipes up, "Oh I'll get your slippers." She goes off and is not seen again. Are there any Naughty, Bossy people here tonight?

Acetate 9 - 10

Last but not least we have Casey Contrary and Lucy Late. Casey Contrary is annoyed because Lucy Late said they could meet up at five o'clock. Well, it was now 5.30 and there was no sign of her. Mind you, it must be said that Lucy Late had actually said she would meet her at 6.30, only that didn't suit Casey Contrary. In fact nothing seemed to suit Casey Contrary. Whenever she was asked to do something she would always want to do the opposite! Do you know anyone like that? I'm sure your mums and dads do sometimes.

Acetate 11

Well, we might not be as bad as some of these characters we have seen but the Bible says that we all have sin in us. Sin is a little word with "I" in the middle. We say wrong things, we do wrong things and we don't like saying "sorry". If God were to look into our hearts at this very moment what would He see? Would He see those nasty thoughts we have about that boy that no-one talks to at school? Would He see the way we treat our brother/sister? The Bible tells us that we can hide nothing from God - He sees everything and everyone! Our hearts are full of Grant Greedys and Gavin Grumpys if we are honest for a moment. How can we ever hope to please God?

Acetate 12

There is only one way and that is to ask Jesus to forgive us for those wrong things we think, say and do. We are told that He will take away all those awful things that keep us apart from God and He will forgive us and become our Friend - the best Friend of all. He makes us clean on the inside and we will become our Friend - the best Friend of all. He makes us clean on the inside and we will become His children.

*(Children are given cards at the end. Each one has a number on one side and a letter on the other. They stand at the front and hold up their cards, one by one. They spell out **Blessed are the pure in heart**.)*

1   Mitch Mean

2 Grant Greedy

3   Nigel Nosey

4 Gavin Grumpy

5 Bart Busy

Beatrice Bossy

7 Naomi Naughty

8   Fiona Fickle

9 Casey Contrary

10 Lucy Late

11 All in a heart

12 Heart

The Race.
(A talk to illustrate man's sin and our need of a Saviour)

I want to tell you about a very important race which takes place once in a life time in a country called Raceland. Everybody takes running very seriously in this country from the youngest to the oldest. Nobody got anywhere without a few races to their credit. To start with races were fairly easy but the strongest and keenest trained for the Big Race - known in some places as the Human Race.

Let's take a closer look at the runners lining up.

Acetate 1

In Lane 1 we have Manfred
In Lane 2 Huw
In Lane 3 Hosea
In Lane 4 Jeff
In Lane 5 Candy
In Lane 6 Cynthia
In Lane 7 Christopher
In Lane 8 Percy

They all look fairly similar but there is one **big** difference between them all. Could you spot it? Well, some will be winners and others losers but you can't always tell at the start. Let's take a closer look - there are other differences - perhaps you can spot them?

In Lane 1 we see Manfred Kind - Man Kind for short. Well what's wrong with Man? Yes, he's facing the wrong way and doesn't even realise it! He won't get far will he?

In Lane 2 Huw Manity has thrown away the letter they were all given from the Great Trainer. Huw thinks he knows it all - he certainly does not need to read this letter. He does not need any outside help thank you very much. He'll manage this race on his own.

In Lane 3 Hosea Pluss - Ho Pluss for short. He is lame so any progress he will make will be slow. Slow but steady - that's his motto.

In Lane 4 Jeff Asakoot cannot hear very well as he always plays really loud music on his walkman. He didn't even take a letter - he thought someone was trying to sell him something!

In Lane 5 Candy Tsee has poor eyesight and has to wear dark glasses as the sun hurts.

In Lane 6 Cynthia Full - Cyn Full for short decides to carry her big rucksack just in case she gets into bother. She has her sleeping bag and emergency survival kit inside. She had kept the letter from the Great Trainer but would probably never find it again as she has so many pockets in her rucksack. She only wants to run downhill - it's easier.

In Lane 7 we see Christopher Tian - He was quite nervous but was determined to do well.

In Lane 8 Percy Verance the good friend of Christopher. They have both put their letters in their body belts so they won't lose it. They mean to study it well when they have chance. They both know they need the Great Trainer's help to complete the race in one piece (or two in their case)

The letter offered to all participants was marked 'For the weak and desperate.' Many of the runners were too proud to even accept it. Percy and Christopher were quite nervous as they had heard stories of people who never came back. Let's see how they get on.

Acetate 2

Man Kind and Huw Manity took the Broad Road as they thought the Narrow Road sounded to difficult. They disappeared and were never seen again.

Acetate 3

Ho Pluss made very slow progress indeed but he felt sure he would get there in the end.

Acetate 4

Jeff Asakoot was running quite well until he got to the quicksand. Some of his fellow runners had shouted out to warn him but he didn't hear them of course as his music was too loud. He got into difficulties and was never seen again.

Acetate 5

Candy Tsee was running quite well for someone with limited sight but didn't see the sign 'Danger Cliff Edge' - Well I'm sure you can imagine what happened.

Acetate 6
Cyn Full can't face going uphill specially with her heavy load. She takes all the downhill paths and heads unknowingly for the Bottomless Ravine.

Acetate 7
Soon Christopher and Percy reach the sign 'Broad Road' 'Narrow Road' They are not sure which road to take so they look carefully at the Trainer's letter. Percy feels they should take the Narrow Road. Christopher is undecided - after all it could be dangerous. Surely they would be a lot safer on the Broad Road. Suddenly Christopher notices one of the instructions written in the letter. It said 'Run with Percy Verance the race marked out for us'.
Well, he would take the road Percy had chosen - dangerous or not! Once on the Narrow Road, although they had to be careful as it was worn in places, it was clearly marked out just like it said in the letter. Sometimes the going got tough and the road became steep and rocky. They soon learned not to look down too much (especially at the drop below them) but looked ahead. Sometimes they thought they caught a glimpse of a figure ahead of them. They believed it was the Trainer himself. They followed the map drawn out for them and obeyed the instructions. They rested by quiet waters and ate at the tables prepared for them. Well, they did finish the race and were rewarded by the Trainer himself. They had never met him before but there were many legends about his great kindness and strength. He gave them their own copy of 'The Runner's Manual' and told them to go back to Raceland and read it every day. They couldn't wait to tell everyone about what had happened to them and how they had actually met the Great Trainer himself. Christopher and Percy soon realised after reading some of the Manual that they had only managed to run the race because the Trainer had gone ahead of them. They owed him their lives. They were determined to tell as many people as they could about him - sometimes they were seen at the start of the Big Race giving out the Trainer's letters and begging the runners to accept and read them. About this time Christopher became more widely known as Chris Tian.

Acetate 8
Well you may be wondering what this story has got to do with you and me? Did you know that we are all in a race - we are part of the Human Race. The Bible says that all of us are facing the wrong direction, we are blind, deaf, lame, and sinful. Not physically of course but we are blind to God's promises and deaf to his laws and we do not listen to the warnings in the Bible. You see in our story those who didn't read the letter for the weak and desperate got lost, or worse, disappeared.
We must all read His word to find out how we can face in the right direction. To run in God's Race we must face the right way (not like Man Kind). How can we make sure we are going the right way? Well, the Bible tells us we must ask Jesus to forgive us for the wrong things that we have done, make us new people and face us in the right direction with our back to our sins and our face towards Heaven. Before we ask Him this we need to realise that we are facing the wrong direction. The Trainer in our story was a picture of Jesus who lived a perfect life and died a perfect death for those who believe.

Acetate 9
You see we cannot reach God by any other way, not by good works, going to church or reading the Bible. Man Kind and Huw Manity thought they could run the race their own way - they were wrong. It is only when we trust in Jesus can we please God and face in the right direction. Which way are you facing? Are you running yet in God's Race?

Children's Song - adapted by C.E. Lusk
to the tune of Chariots of Fire.

Come run in God's Race,
Come all blind and lame,
Come follow the Champion,
Christ Jesus His Name.
I ask you Lord Jesus, fulfil my desire,
Oh bless me and make me a chariot of fire.
Forgive all my sins, Lord Jesus Christ
My Lord and My Saviour,
Come run by my side and I will be a chariot of fire.

1   Human race

3   Ho Pluss

Cyn Full

7   Christopher & Percy

8   The Bible

9   The Bridge

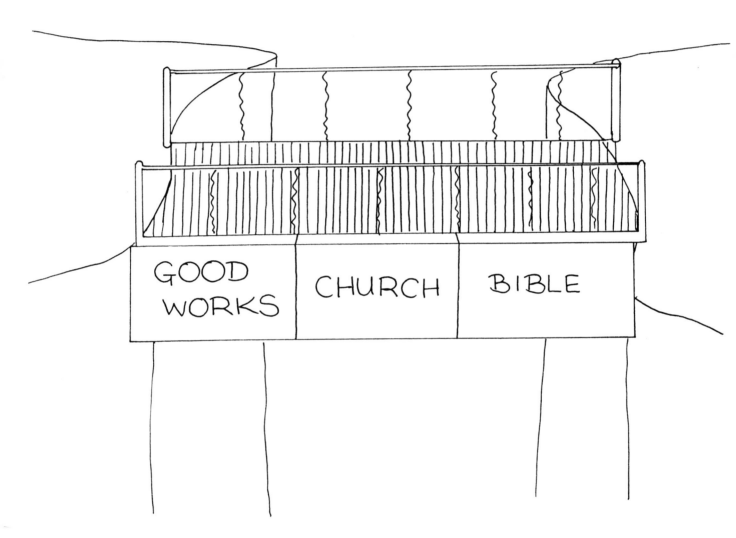

Tommy Terror and Gordon Goodtoall
(A talk to illustrate the substitutionary death of Christ)

Acetate 1

Once upon a time there was a boy called Tommy - nothing unusual about that you may say but his surname was Terror and it was a question of Terror by name and terror by nature! Let me explain.

Tommy was a very naughty boy who always did naughty things. You can see the sort of things he did in the pictures. He chased little girls to pull their hair and he called others by nasty names which sometimes made them cry. I hope there aren't any Tommy Terrors listening to this story!

Oh dear, Tommy just got worse and worse. He just didn't know when to stop. He spat at others - yuk - and hit them with whatever he could lay his hands on. Of course he only ever picked on people smaller than himself and he always made sure that they did not have any older brothers or sisters.

Acetate 2

Well, Tommy had a cousin called Gordon Goodtoall who was the complete opposite of him. Gordon often used to feel uneasy at his cousin's awful behaviour towards other boys and girls at his school. Tommy was always getting in trouble both at school and at home.

Acetate 3

One day during a maths lesson Tommy did a really naught thing. He and Gordon were sitting on the front row when all of a sudden Tommy got out his catapult while the teacher's back was turned and launched a rubber into space. With a sickening thud it hit the back of the teacher's head! Oh no! This time Tommy had gone too far! The teacher slowly turned around to face the class, his face bright red and the veins standing out on his neck! He was very, very angry. No-one had ever seen him so mad. He yelled at the class so loudly that they thought the windows would shatter. "Who did it? Own up now or else!" A deep silence followed - even Tommy held his breath. Everyone looked wide eyed at the teacher Mr Thrashum. Slowly Gordon put up his hand - he was shaking with Fear. "So it was you Goodtoall! How dare you! Wait till your parents find out about this. You'll get it from them as well! Bend over." Gordon did what he was told. The class looked on in horror - Tommy looked the most shocked of them all. Everyone winced as Gordon's howls filled the air.

Acetate 4

Why did Gordon take the punishment that was due to Tommy? He told Tommy it was because he was a Christian and he didn't want to see Tommy expelled from the school. Tommy had already been warned by the Headteacher that if he continued to break school rules then he would no longer be allowed to come to this school. Tommy still did not understand so Gordon told him another story which might make more sense.

Many years ago there lived a man who lived a perfect life. He spent his time thinking of others and not about himself. He healed the sick and even raised people from the dead. He was no ordinary man.

Acetate 5

He made many enemies who did not like to see all the good he was doing. They hated him so much that they invented cruel stories about him. Others believed the cruel lies and they ended up killing him. In fact he was laughed at, punched, whipped and spat upon. Finally he was nailed to a cross and died an agonising death.

Why did he do all that if he was innocent? Well, the Bible tells us that Jesus took the punishment that was due to us for all the bad things that we have done in our lives. Can you think of some bad things that you have done? Well, if you ask God to forgive you He will because Jesus has already been punished in your place.

That was not the end of the story because after Jesus died and was buried he arose from the dead. This showed everyone that God was very very pleased with all that Jesus had done to save lost sinners.

Acetate 6
Tommy wiped away his tears and realised for the first time what it meant that Jesus had died in his place. Gordon had spoken to him before about Jesus but he used to tell him to shut up. He thanked Gordon for taking the cane in his place and decided there and then that with God's help he would no longer live up to his name of Terror.

What about you? You might not have done so many awful things like Tommy but you still need Jesus to forgive you. What will you do?

1   Tommy Terror & little girl

2   Gordon Goodtoall

3   Maths Lesson

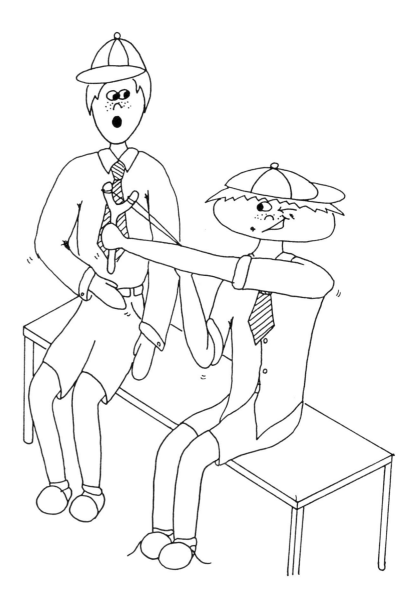

4 Gordon's Punishment

5 The Cross

6 Tommy & Gordon

Timothy and Tommy Trouble
(A talk to illustrate the substitutionary death of Christ)

Acetate 1.
Timothy and Thomas Trouble were identical twins - like peas in a pod they were. The only way you could tell them apart was that Tim wore glasses and had slightly darker hair. Tom's hair was more gingery and he had freckles. However, they were very different in other aspects.
Tim loved to read - Tommy loved to watch T.V.
Acetate 2.
Tim hated sport - Tom loved it. Sometimes they played tennis together but Tom would always win and Tim would walk off in a huff.
Acetate 3.
Tim loved doing sums and loved to remember dates in history.
Tom liked building things. His latest model was a boat which sank!
Acetate 4.
There was one thing that Tom was very very good at and that was computers! He would spend hours on his computer at home and at Computer Club at School.
Acetate 5.
Exam time came around all too quickly for Tom. Tim did really well in most of his subjects. He always worked hard. Tom tried his best but he never did very well. He was a little jealous of his twin Tim. Tom found it hard to keep awake in some exams and lessons. He just wasn't that interested.
Acetate 6A
One day Tom got an idea. Now his teachers did not write out school reports any more - they were all typed up on computers and printed out. Well, one lunchtime while at Computer Club he managed to get access into the school report file and suddenly on the screen at the press of a button he saw his own report and that of Tim's. He read them eagerly. As usual Tim's report was glowing and his was average. What if he changed the names at the top of the reports? No one would know and he would get a good report for once! Tom checked that his teacher was busy with someone else and tapped a few buttons and there it was - done! *(show acetate 6B)*
Acetate 7.
Tim was very upset when he saw his report! He had worked so hard - he just didn't understand what had gone wrong.
Tom leapt for joy when he saw his report! His parents were delighted. They thought he had at last turned over a new leaf.
Tim's parents were upset with him and disappointed.
Unknown to Tom, Mrs Trouble had written a short letter to school - to the headteacher - saying how pleased she was with Tom's excellent progress but how disappointed they were with Tim's report.
Acetate 8.
Anyway, to cut a long story short - Tom was well and truly found out! His parents were angry with him and so was his headteacher. He now wished he had never thought of doing such a thing!
After everyone had calmed down his parents had a long talk with Tom. They told him they loved him as he was. He did not have to try and be someone he wasn't. Tom felt very sad and ashamed of his bad behaviour and so he said he was very sorry.
God knows all about us. We cannot hide anything from Him because He sees everyone and everything. He sees us at school and at home and with our friends. We cannot even pretend we are different to what we are really like deep down. Imagine if God were to write a report for us at the end of our life or even if we could see what had been written about us so far...
Acetate 9A.
Perhaps it would look something like this:- *read out and display first report with ME written at the top)*
What an awful report! Do some of these things sound familiar? Could we put our name at the top of that page without having to alter much? Would we have passed or failed the test of life? Well, according to this we would have failed! *(Cover up word **fail** till last moment)*
Some people might think we are good boys and girls - our teachers perhaps or our aunts and uncles. They don't always see us on our bad days. Only those closest to us know about them! Of course God sees us on our good

days and our bad days. Our good days are not always **that** good though are they? Be honest! There has only ever been one person who got a good report from God with no bad comments at all. Do you know who that was? It was Jesus, God's Son. Let's imagine the sort of things God would have written about His Son Jesus.
Acetate 9B.
(Show 2nd report and read out - keep 'pass' covered)
The list is endless but I stopped here. If a real report on Jesus was written I thing they would run out of paper before they ran out of good things to say! I would much rather have a report like this, wouldn't you? This is a most definite pass. How could I ever get such a good report from God? - it would be impossible - especially as the pass mark in the test of life is 100%! I suppose I could swop over the names like Tom did and pretend the good report belonged to me. Do you think I could fool God? No I don't think so somehow!
The Bible tells us that Jesus died a horrible death on a cross because wicked people would not believe He was who He said He was. They hated Him although He had only loved people and spent time with them. We are told in the Bible that Jesus was punished in our place - he took the punishment for all the bad things we have done. *(Refer back to Report One)*
Do you know what God will do if we say sorry to Him for all the wrong things we have done and thank Jesus for dying in our place? He does something amazing! It's as if He crosses out our name at the top of our report and writes Jesus' name and crosses out Jesus' name and writes ours! *(Show report 9C & 9D)*
How can this be? Well, if you get a bad report from school you may be punished. Jesus was punished for all the wrong things **we** have done. There is no more punishment left for those who turn to Jesus. If we come to Jesus and ask Him to forgive us God no longer sees all the bad things in our lives. He only sees all the good things His Son has done. God reads our report as if it were His Son's!
The Bible says we will all have a sort of report from God at the end of our life. The question is - whose name will appear at the top? If it is only our name we will have failed the test and will not be allowed into Heaven. However, if God has put Jesus' name there instead of ours because we have said sorry to Him then we will be welcomed into His Heaven and be with Him forever.
Read out John 3v16.

1   Timmy reading & Tommy watching TV

2   Tennis

3   Sums & Boat building

4   Tom's Computer

5   Exam Time

6A

SCHOOL REPORT
NAME:-   TIMOTHY TROUBLE

Subject	Comment
Maths	Very good
English	Excellent
Science	Superb work
History	Excellent
Geography	Very good
P.E.	Satisfactory
I.T.	Quite good

SCHOOL REPORT
NAME:-   THOMAS TROUBLE

Subject	Comment
Maths	Poor
English	Weak
Science	Poor
History	Quite good
Geography	Weak
P.E.	Very good
I.T.	Good

6B

SCHOOL REPORT
NAME:-   THOMAS TROUBLE

Subject	Comment
Maths	Very good
English	Excellent
Science	Superb work
History	Excellent
Geography	Very good
P.E.	Satisfactory
I.T.	Quite good

SCHOOL REPORT
NAME:-   TIMOTHY TROUBLE

Subject	Comment
Maths	Poor
English	Weak
Science	Poor
History	Quite good
Geography	Weak
P.E.	Very good
I.T.	Good

7   Tim & Tom

8 Tom

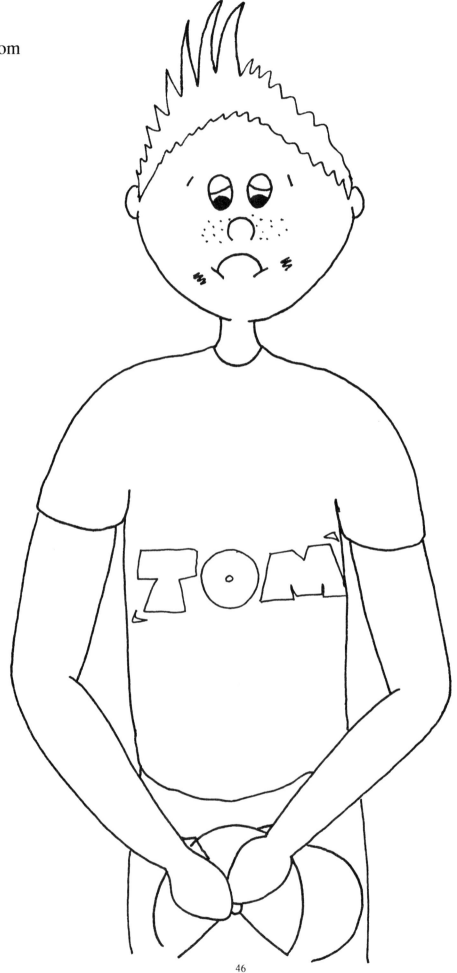

9A
LIFE REPORT
NAME:-   **ME**

Helps with the washing up if asked!
Shares toys - Sometimes
Loses temper - Often
Thinks spiteful things - Sometimes
Lies to parents if in trouble
Disobeys mum and dad
Shows off if can't have own way...

Pass
FAIL

9B
SCHOOL REPORT
NAME:-   **JESUS**

Loved people
Spent time with friends
Obeyed his parents
Always patient
Never had tantrums
Served God
Wanted always to do God's will
Told others about his heavenly Father
Never hit back
Always shared all he ever had
Gave to the poor
helped the lonely

PASS
Fail

9C
LIFE REPORT
NAME:-   **JESUS**

Helps with the washing up if asked!
Shares toys - Sometimes
Loses temper - Often
Thinks spiteful things - Sometimes
Lies to parents if in trouble
Disobeys mum and dad
Shows off if can't have own way...

Pass
FAIL

9D
SCHOOL REPORT
NAME:-   **ME**

Loved people
Spent time with friends
Obeyed his parents
Always patient
Never had tantrums
Served God
Wanted always to do God's will
Told others about his heavenly Father
Never hit back
Always shared all he ever had
Gave to the poor
helped the lonely

PASS
Fail

Sammy's Special Day
(The Good Shepherd - John 10)

Acetate 1. 'Wake up, wake up, let's go, let's go into the hills. It's 6 o'clock in the morning - quick before it gets too hot!' shouted Sammy at the top of his voice. His brother Michael was still half asleep. Today was a special day. Sammy's brothers were taking him up into the hills to see the lambs. He and his family had a sheep farm. When he grew up he wanted to be a shepherd like his brothers. You had to be very brave and strong to be a shepherd where Sammy lived.

Acetate 2. Usually as Sammy was the youngest he would stay at home and help his mum run the farm. He loved playing out with his friends Becky and Esther. His favourite game was blind man's bluff!

Acetate 3. As soon as he had had his breakfast and had dressed they set off together - little Sammy and his four brothers. They used to tease him sometimes and call him 'Shorty' but he didn't really mind. He loved to be with his brothers.

Acetate 4. He loved it at night on the mountains especially when they gathered around the camp fire, his eyes sparkling as he listened to their exciting shepherd stories. There were still lots of wild animals around those parts of the mountains.

Once one of his brothers had to fight off a lion who wanted to kill the sheep. He learned how important it was to protect the sheep at all costs and how weak and defenceless they were too.

Acetate 5. Sometimes thieves tried to steal them. The brothers had to keep watch.

Acetate 6. They were also rather stupid and never took any notice of danger signs - as long as there was plenty of lush green grass! Many times a sheep has fallen over a cliff edge and ended up being stuck on a ledge... his brother would wait until the bleating got weaker before he attempted to rescue him. Whenever the life of a sheep was saved the brothers were delighted.

Acetate 7. The story he loved to hear was the one about his older brother Tommy. On a cold winter's night he noticed that one of the lambs had disappeared. The lamb's mother was bleating loudly but to no avail. It was very cold, even the stream had frozen - but there was nothing for it he went out to look for him. His mother tried to persuade him to wait until morning but Tommy knew that in such low temperatures the little lamb would not survive. He searched and searched high and low when it began to snow. He called out and whistled, hoping he would be recognised. Suddenly he heard a faint bleat and followed it. The lamb had fallen into a trap meant for bears. It was a deep hole - there was no way he could get him out without help - so he tied his red handkerchief to the bush near the pit and used a rope to lower himself down.

Acetate 8. The little lamb was very cold. He cuddled him and calmed him down. He could feel the warmth creeping back into his body.

In the morning he was found by his other brothers - just in time - they had to take him to the doctor's as he nearly died. The little lamb was fine, a little shaky, but Tommy had to be carried down.

Sammy loved this story - it reminded him of some of the Bible stories Jesus told. It reminded him that he acted like a silly sheep sometimes and needed Jesus to be his shepherd and protect him from the dangers around him. Once again secretly in his heart he said 'Thank you Lord Jesus for saving me from my sin.'

Acetate 9. Did you know the Bible says we are like sheep in God's sight?

What, like dirty, smelly, stupid sheep? Yes. We all prefer to do our own thing, live our own lives rather than follow Jesus. A hopeless situation, or is it?

Well it would have been unless Jesus had become the good shepherd who laid down his life - how? It was a bit like what Tommy did to save the little lamb on that dark night, except that Jesus did actually die in our place on the cross. Jesus came as a baby - no ordinary baby - a very special one. He was God's only Son and he came willingly to rescue those who needed rescuing. If we turn to him and ask him to forgive the wrong things we have done, the Bible tells us that he will rescue us and make us his children.

Are we going to carry on being foolish sheep or are we going to ask Jesus our shepherd to forgive us and rescue us?

1   Sammy & Michael

2   Sammy Playing

3   Sammy and his Brothers

4 Brother with lion

5   Sheep thief

6   Sheep in danger

7   Tommy looking for his sheep

8   Tommy with lamb

9 Sheep and lamb

Freddy Fantastic's Firework Factory
(A talk for Bonfire Night)

What are your favourite fireworks?

Well, I am going to tell you about something strange that happened one night a few days before Bonfire night at Freddy Fantastic's Firework Factory.

The air was electric in the factory that night. Tension had been mounting noticeably over the past few days. You see the fireworks had been arguing and squabbling among themselves about who was the best firework. Sparks had begun to fly!

1. Rock Hit - the sky rocket spokesman boasted they could go higher than any other firework and could fill the sky with their spectacular showers of glittering sparks. They tended to look down on the other fireworks.
2. Vince Volcano erupted as usual and shot down Rock Hit in flames. He was the spokesman for all the Roman candles and Glitter Fountains. He boasted that they were the best because they were the most colourful and were quieter and gentler than the sky rockets.
3. Craig Crackle was a bit of a bright spark and so spoke up for the sparklers. They were by far the prettiest and safest of fireworks and they brought much joy and happiness to children.
4. Catherine Wheel was the spokeswoman for herself. She did not say much but went round in circles a lot.
5. Bett Spring was the spokeswoman for the Jumping Jacks. They were the best because they moved the quickest.
6. Ed Banger was the spokesman for all the bangers and sky bombs. They were the best because they made the loudest noise and were a lot of fun to be with.

Who do you think was the best firework?

Bonfire Night came and went - no sooner was the sky alight with dazzling rockets than it was once again dark - that's the trouble with fireworks - they only last for a short time.

Did you know that we have a lot in common with fireworks? Some of us are a bit like the Rock Hits, Vince Volcanos, Craig Crackles, Catherine Wheels, Bett Springs and Ed Bangers of my story.
- Some of us are like Rock Hit who look down on some people - proud.
- Some of us have short fuses like Vince Volcano.
- Some of us say and do some silly things like Craig Crackle.
- Some of us spend our days going round in circles like a Catherine Wheel - wasting time - not doing much at all.
- Some of us are like Bett Spring and Jumping Jacks - up one minute, down the next - very moody.
- Some of us are like Ed Banger and his friends - we just like to make a lot of noise to impress people or frighten/bully people.

The Bible tells us that we act like this because of <u>sin</u> in our lives. The Bible also tells us that <u>no</u> sinful person will be able to go to heaven. The Bible reminds us that our life is like a mist, a puff of smoke - even the oldest person in the world will have to leave this life one day. What are we going to do with the life we have - short though it may be - just like a firework?

7. Look at these poor fireworks - a few minutes into Bonfire night - black - empty - dirty. Do you know that when God looks at us the Bible says we look as dirty as an old firework - because of all the wrong things we have done. What hope is there for us? How can we who are dirty inside become clean? The Bible also says that those who trust Jesus and have said sorry to him for all the wrong they have done will one day glisten like jewels in heaven - forever. I would rather be like a glistening jewel than like an old charred firework, wouldn't you?

There is a little rhyme that people say on 5th November - do you know what it is?
> Remember, remember the 5th of November,
> Gunpowder, treason and plot.

8. Well the Bible also has a verse which starts with Remember, and its aimed at people your age - children and young people.

'Remember your Creator in the days of your youth'   *Ecclesiastes 12v1.*

Never forget that Jesus can be your best Friend of all if you come to him and thank him for dying in your place on the cross.

1   Rock Hit

2   Vince Volcano

3   Craig Crackle

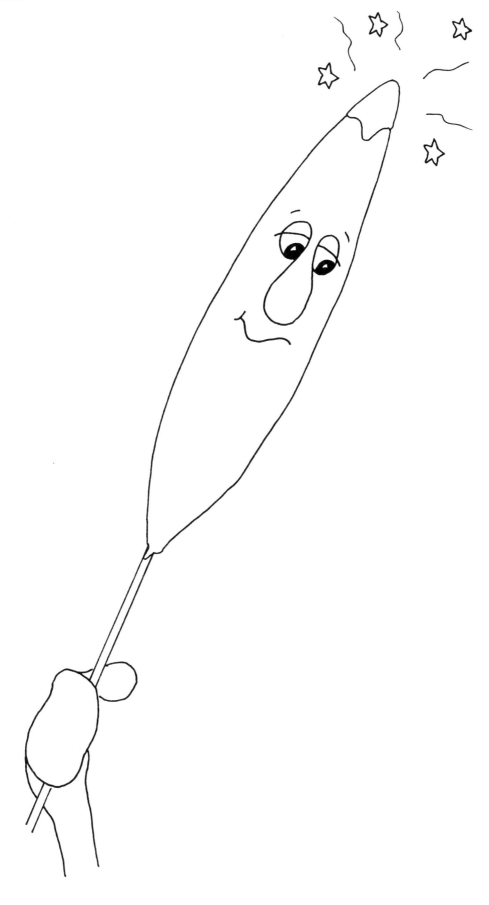

4   Catherine Wheel

5   Bett Spring

6 Ed Banger

7 All the used Fireworks

Remember your creator

in the days

of your youth.

Ecclesiastes 12 v 1.

Suzy's Christmas
(A Seasonal Story)

Acetate 1

Suzy was so excited. It was Christmas Eve and her mum was in hospital having a baby. Would it be a boy or a girl? She wanted a sister but had decided that she would still be pleased if it was a boy. She didn't feel tired at all although it was late. Christmas was a good time to have a baby.

She eventually fell asleep and early next morning she was awakened by Aunty Helen who told her she had a baby sister. Wow! A little sister! She couldn't wait to tell her friends.

Acetate 2

So straight after breakfast Aunty Helen drove Suzy to the hospital. It took a long time because there were a lot of other cars on the road. Suzy fell asleep, tired after her late night and early rising.

Acetate 3

In her dream she saw a young man standing next to a young woman. The young woman looked very thoughtful at what the man said to her. She said, "I will do whatever God wants."

Acetate 4

Next she saw the same young woman but this time she was expecting a baby. She was travelling with an older man who must have been her husband. Poor lady looked very tired.

They had arrived at the town and tried to find somewhere to stay but all the guest houses and hotels were full up. What would they do? It looked like the baby would be born very soon.

Acetate 5

In the end they found a stable. The baby was born and wrapped in strips of cloth and laid in a cattle trough. Poor little thing! Yet the baby seemed quite content. They even had a visit from some local shepherds who told them wonderful stories of angels appearing to them while they were in the fields with their sheep. They knew that their little baby was no ordinary child. He was the Christ who had long ago been promised. They were amazed as they looked on the tiny wriggling body before them. Could this really be the Saviour of the world? Yet the angels had spoken with such authority. It must be true!

Acetate 6

Suzy wakes up just as they draw in to the hospital. She rushes up the steps to see her mum and new baby sister. Her mum looked so happy as she sat in bed nursing Beth. Suzy thought about her dream and remembered the look on Mary's face. There was no draughty stable here but a nice warm bed. Suzy said a prayer to Jesus as she stood next to her mum's bed. "Happy Birthday Jesus! Thank you for my little sister but thank you most of all for Yourself - the best Christmas Present of all!"

1   Suzy and the Christmas Tree

2   Suzy in the car

3   Mary and the Angel

4   Mary and Joseph

5   Mary, Joseph and Jesus

6   Suzy and her mum

The Prince and the Teenie Weenies
(A Christmas Story)

Once upon a time a long time ago in a land called Micropotania lived a people called the Teenie Weenies. They thought they knew everything - they were very stuck up and very proud of being Teenie Weenies. They didn't believe in the existence of any other people - there were many fairytales and stories of another land beyond the Far Mountains, but they said only children and the superstitious believed these stories! The Weenies were actually very small - no more than a metre high. The funny thing was - they thought they were the tallest and best in the whole world! What did they do?

Acetate 1

They danced and had parties.
They fought each other and argued quite a lot.

Acetate 2

They were not religious but worshipped big houses, smart clothes, beautiful cars.

Acetate 3

Some people were different... They would meet in each other's houses a couple of times a week, sing songs and listen to stories. They believed that there was a King - a great King from beyond the Far Mountains who would one day visit them and help them. They used to meet to pray to their great King to ask him to come quickly and rescue them.

Acetate 4

Everyone else thought they were mad. They were nicknamed 'Kinglings'. People turned up their noses even higher at these poor people. Some 'Kinglings' had been attacked and some had been killed by the Teenie mobs. Some 'Kinglings' were thrown into jail because they loved to sing about their King. Some were even burnt in big fires.

Let's go and see if there is a King beyond the Far Mountains, and let's leave the Teenies to their weenie small minded ways.

Acetate 5

What a beautiful country, everything shone with gold. There were magnificent mansions where lots of happy people lived - These were for the 'Kinglings' who had run away from Micropotania to find the Golden City in the Far Away land for themselves. They were no longer 'Teenies' or 'Kinglings' but were now Children of the King (kings and queens themselves), each with their own crown.

Acetate 6

They loved to spend time with the Prince and the King.
They loved to listen to his wonderful stories and loved to worship him.
It was a wonderful place. Laughter and song filled the air.

Acetate 7

The great King and his son Prince Lionheart were very sad at the way the Teenies lived out their miserable little lives without hardly ever lifting their eyes to the Far Away Mountains or wondering why they were there. The great King had given messages to his friends the Kinglings - warnings too, and a book - a special book to read which contained the King's story. The great King was a good king and hated all the wrong things the Teenies had done. He had made them and had placed them in their land many years before. They had broken his laws and even tried to destroy the King's Book. Yet the King and his son the Prince loved these strange little people! What could be done to put things right once and for all and show the teenies what they were missing and how much they were loved?

The King and the Prince talked and talked about what could be done. One day the King had an idea and whispered it to the Prince. It seemed incredible, almost impossible! The incredible plan was soon announced to everyone. It was simply amazing - no one could even have dreamed of it!

The only way for the Teenies to really understand the King's love would be for the Prince to become a Teenie himself. What, how could the great and noble Prince Lionheart himself become a Teenie Weenie? How could he stoop so low?

How could this be possible?

Acetate 8

Well, the great King and his son can do what they want as they had great power. So the plans were made, the

Prince said his farewells. The people of the Golden City felt sad at seeing their Prince leave but he did promise to come back soon. So the great Prince was shrunk down to Teenie size and was born to a young Teenie girl.

Acetate 9

Uncle Bob looked up from the flickering flames and glanced at the eager faces around him.

'What happened when he was born?' asked Sophie. 'Did anyone know that he was really the great Prince?'

Tom butted in: 'I hope those teenies looked after that little baby'.

Uncle Bob smiled and picked up a big book and said 'Let me read you something from the great King's story book - Oh yes, we call it The Bible.'

Acetate 10

One day a young girl called Mary who was engaged to Joseph received a very strange visitor - an angel who told her that she was going to have a baby - a special baby - the son of God! She was amazed but believed it to be true. A short while later Jesus was born in an outhouse in Bethlehem because there was no room in the guest house.

Acetate 11

Their first visitors were a group of shepherds who told them about the wonderful things that had happened to them. An angel had appeared to them and had told them about the special new baby called Jesus because he would save his people from their sins.

Acetate 12

When Jesus was a bit older they were visited by some wise men from a far away country. They had followed a star which led them to the house where Joseph and Mary were living. They brought beautiful but strange gifts for a baby, myrrh, frankincense and gold!

Mary wondered and thought a lot about all these events.

You see children - Christmas is a very special time - it's not just about giving and buying presents for mums and dads, aunties and uncles. Let us never forget that Jesus (the great Prince of our story) is the greatest gift of all! Just think, Jesus who was there right at the beginning of time, who created the stars and the moon, the earth and us, became a little tiny baby so he could grow up, become a man and die in the place of us sinners! What an amazing story, but this one is true! Will you accept Jesus, not as a tiny baby, but as your Friend and Rescuer who died for your sins?

1   Dancing and Fighting

2   Car

3   Prayer

4   Jail

5   Golden City

6 Prince

7   The King

8   The Prince's farewell

9   Uncle Bob

10 Angel and Mary

11 Shepherd

12   Wise Men

Noah's Flood

(A talk to illustrate God's judgement and His provision of a Saviour)

Introduction
Props:- bin-liner full of various items eg. umbrella, wellies, waterproof jacket, rain hat, weather forecast etc.

I am going to tell you about a land which was very different from our own. In fact it was so different it could have been another world - well it almost was. There were some things that you would never have found in the shops of this land. You could have searched high and low and still not come across them. I have some of these things in this bag. Can you guess what they are? I'll give you a clue - the reason you wouldn't find these things is because no-one had need of them. (Give some other clues if you want) If they'd had newspapers in those days then you would never have found one of these (hold up a weather forecast). No-one ever talked about the weather - do you know why? Well, this land was very different from our own because IT NEVER RAINED! The climate was sunny and warm. The earth was covered by lush forests including the North and South Poles! There was no snow, no ice, no severe storms and no deserts. What a beautiful world it must have been! Animals grew much bigger in those days and lived longer. The fossil record shows us that there were dragonflies which measured 30 inches (75cms) across their wings! There were 12 inch cockroaches! There were also very large animals called dinosaurs which often measured 50ft (15m) long. Some flying reptiles had a wingspan of 50ft (15m). What's more, people lived a lot longer in those days. Many lived into their 900s! Do you know how old the oldest man was? Methuselah was 969 years old.

Acetate 1
In other ways this land was very much like ours. People fought each other and stole from each other. They drank too much and ate too much. There was so much evil in the world that God became sad and began to wish that He had never created man!

Acetate 2
However, there was a good man who pleased God and his name was Noah. He and his wife and family were probably farmers. God decides to wipe mankind off the face of the earth as well as all the animals and birds. God tells Noah His plan like one friend confiding in another. He tells him to build a big boat - huge boat:- 450ft (140m), 75ft wide (23) and 45ft tall (13.5m). He was to make an opening for light across the top, include three decks for animal stalls and storage and a door in the side. It would be ENORMOUS! It has been calculated that there would have been enough room for 432 double decker buses! There was enough room for pairs of all living animals and dinosaurs. It was big enough to carry 50,000 animals. The ark would have looked more like a giant cargo ship or like an enclosed barge. The ark was covered inside and out with pitch to make everything watertight.

Acetate 3
So what did Noah say after God had told him what to do? Did he make excuses like "I'm not skilled enough to build a big boat" or "What will other people say when they see what I am doing - they'll think I'm mad!"
Noah didn't say any of these things but we are told that he did everything just as God commanded him.
He began to build this big boat. You can imagine what the locals thought. They must have laughed at him and his family many times. Why build such a huge boat in the middle of dry land? It took 120 years to build it. How everyone must have jeered at Noah - they probably made up jokes about him too. Noah carried on doing what God had asked him to do. He even took the time to preach to them to warn them to seek God's mercy. That made them laugh all the more no doubt! They lived their lives and got married and had children and ate and drank. They carried on ignoring God and His servant Noah.
We all have rules to follow in our lives don't we? Can you think of some school rules? Some are easier to follow than others. Do you know that many years after Noah, God gave us a special set of 10 rules. What were they called? How many have you kept? The Bible tells us that we have not kept God's laws, we have sinned and deserve to be punished just like the people of Noah's day. They didn't care about God or His workers. What about us? Do we make God sad when He sees our thoughts and actions.

Acetate 4
Well, one day 120 years later the last nail was knocked in and the last bucket of pitch used up. The ark was ready. It probably looked something like this here (4a) rather than this (4b). So the animals began to arrive because God was bringing them to the ark from all over. There were two of every kind of air-breathing animals male and female.

Acetate 5
I am sure there were some animals that are not alive today such as dinosaurs. Some dinosaurs grew up to 80ft long so perhaps Noah took young dinosaurs on board to make it a little more comfortable for the other travellers. What a sight it must have been to see all the animals turning up and standing in line waiting to get on board. Once they were all safely inside God shut the door. Seven days later the biggest storm in history began and raged for 40 days and 40 nights. Feeding all those animals probably wasn't such a major task if many of them went into hibernation. Bears hibernate when the weather is bad and almost every creature will lie down very quiet and still when trapped and during times of danger. The great storm would have been very frightening as the winds howled and the thunder crashed and the waves billowed. There were probably earthquakes too. "On that day all the fountains of the great deep were broken up and the windows of heaven were opened." Genesis 7v11. All the water above the earth and below the earth would have rushed to cover it. The ground would have split open and great geysers of water, lava and steam would have gushed out. Some scientists believe that large meteors fell at this time too leaving huge craters. The world quickly became one huge ocean. The rain went on and on - perhaps Noah wondered whether it would ever stop but he continued to count the days 38, 39, 40, 41 - a sunny day, calm at last!

Acetate 6
Soon God sent a wind and the flooding began to disappear. Six months after entering the boat they suddenly felt a bump as the ark came to rest on dry land - actually a mountain called Ararat 17,000ft high (nearly six times bigger than Snowdon or Ben Nevis). Soon the tops of other mountains became visible. Ten weeks later Noah sent out a raven to look for dry land. Then he sends a dove which returns as it can find nowhere to build a nest. Later he sends it out once more and this time it returns with an olive leaf. So now Noah knew that the trees had begun to grow again. A week later he sends out a dove which never returns. They waited a few more weeks for the land to dry out so that the animals may be able to live on it and make their homes. So after a year and ten days Noah and his family and all the animals leave the ark.

Noah builds an altar and makes a sacrifice to God to thank Him for keeping them all safe. God makes a promise never to flood the whole earth again. What sign does God give us as a reminder to us all that He will never flood the earth again? After the flood Noah's diet changed too. Genesis 9v3: "Everything that lives and moves will be food for you. Just as I gave you the green plants, I now give you everything." The earth became a much harsher place to live in after the flood and people did not live so long.

Conclusion
Some people don't believe that a world-wide flood ever happened. We believe it did because the Bible tells us it did. However, many scientists are having to rethink their position on the Genesis flood as the fossil record points at it so clearly. There are fossil graveyards all over the world, and in many, creatures including huge dinosaurs have been preserved. Normally when an animal dies it quickly rots away and does not become a fossil. So all those millions of animals in those fossil graveyards had to be buried fast or they would not be in the rocks now! Only a huge sudden flood could do this. In 1877 in a coal mine in Belgium, fossilised skeletons of 23 Iguanadons were found all piled up together. They were most likely killed and buried by Noah's flood. (Iguanadons weighed between 6-8 tons and were 30ft long and 15ft high).

What has all this about the flood got to do with us today? Well, God still speaks to people through the Bible and one of His commands is "Believe on the Lord Jesus Christ and you will be saved." Are we obedient to God's commands like Noah? God will never again flood the earth, but one day Jesus is going to come back for His people and to punish those who have not asked for His forgiveness. That day will be a terrible day worse than any great flood for those who have lived their lives as they wanted. The Bible helps us to understand how Jesus saves His people by using the story of Noah. If we believe in Jesus we are safe like Noah and his family were in the ark. We are protected from God's anger against sin. "Noah did everything just as God commanded him." What about you?

1 Drunk and gorged

2   Noah and his wife

3   Noah ready to build the Ark

4   The finished Ark

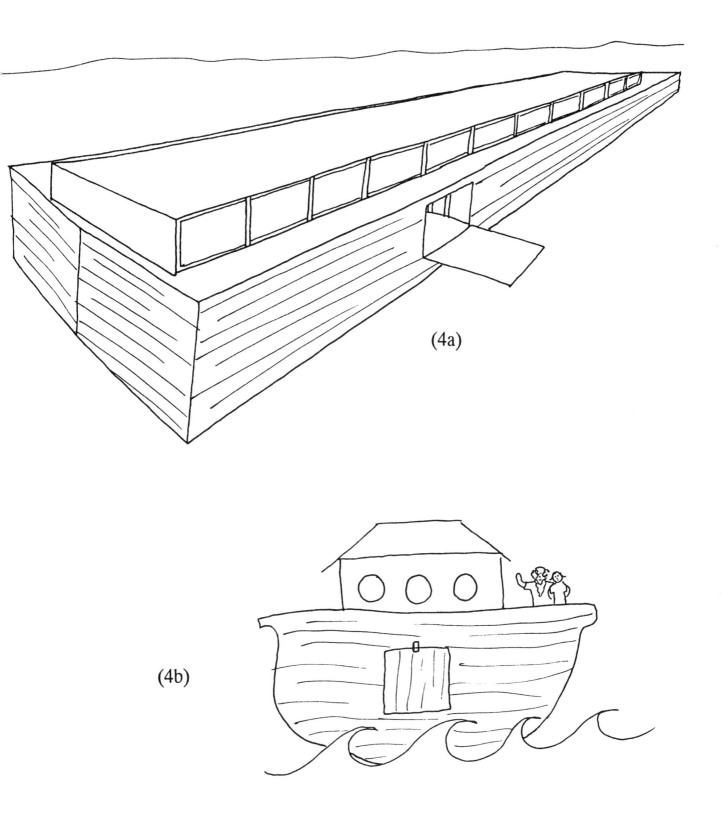

(4a)

(4b)

5   The animals

6   Noah and the animals

Ivor Nopennies and the Hidden Treasure
(Finding the true treasure)

Introduction
Show a bag containing gardening equipment and bucket and spade. Children try and guess what hobby I have and what my favourite occupation on the beach was when I was a little girl. Introduce digging. Whether you dig in the garden or on the beach you can still come across these.... (rocks/stones)

Acetate 1
Our story today is about a man who spent a lot of his day in a field digging and preparing the ground. He was a market gardener but only on a small scale. His name was Mr Nopennies which really suited him because.... yes, he had no money - he was quite poor. His first name was Ivor and he was married to Fancy and they lived in a small cottage in the countryside. Although they were quite poor they were happy with their lot.

Acetate 2
They rented a field from Mr Loadsamoney - a good name for him too seeing as he was the richest farmer in the area.

Ivor was a hard worker and grew all sorts of fruit and veg - can you guess some of the things that he grew? He had green fingers, not just one or two but every finger had a greenish tinge. Whatever he grew was the biggest and the best - his gooseberries were as big and juicy as plums! His strawberries were as big as tomatoes! He even won prizes for his marrows! They were so big it took two people to carry one. Whatever he grew he would sell at the local market. Before he could enjoy his bumper harvests he had to work very hard.

Acetate 3
He would have to prepare the ground and dig and dig before planting his seeds. He had to throw away the rocks and pull up the weeds. He used to often get backache but he knew his efforts would one day be rewarded. One day he was digging away and it was a hot day and the sweat was rolling off him. Suddenly his spade made a clunking noise as it hit something hard. "Oh no, not more stones!" thought Ivor as he wearily bent down to pick them up and throw to one side. Sometimes when digging he would day-dream about owning a big farm like Mr Loadsamoney and paying people to do all the hard work while he supervised from his tractor. After a few minutes of trying to dislodge the stones he realised that something was up. He looked harder and saw an old metal box which had been buried. He scooped it out of the soil and inspected it - the lock was broken so he carefully opened it and guess what he saw inside! Well, he could hardly believe his eyes - he thought his eyes were going to pop out. There were lots and lots of precious jewels and gold rings! They glistened and shone - so many colours - he had never seen anything quite so beautiful. He suddenly grinned from ear to ear and thought: "I'm rich!" Then he began to think that perhaps he wasn't rich after all. The only person who was rich was Mr Loadsamoney. He had done all the work and found the treasure - the farmer would just say "Thank you" and take it all. He didn't know what to do, but sat down and scratched his head. He made a plan. First he buried the treasure again and then tried to act normal as if nothing was wrong. He wanted that treasure more than anything else in the world.

Acetate 4
So off he went home and told his wife that they had far too many possessions and that he was going to sell some to make more room in the house. His wife couldn't believe her eyes as she watched her husband load up his wheelbarrow with their furniture. She thought he had gone mad. This went on for months until they hardly had anything left in the house. He saved up every penny. He even told his wife to only buy the cheapest meat and bread.

One day he plucked up courage and went to see Mr Loadsamoney to ask him if he could buy his field. When the farmer said how much he would accept Ivor nearly fell off his chair. Ivor realised that he would have to save up a lot more money as there was no chance that the greedy farmer would ever lower his price. There was a rumour that before he had become a farmer he had set up a business of skinning bees for their fur!

So Ivor went home and thought about what else he could sell to raise the money - any ideas? Well, the carpets went, his clothes went and then he had another idea - he sold his house! By this time his poor wife was close to tears and wondered if Ivor had some serious illness that was making him act in such a strange way - he was definitely not himself! All his friends thought he was mad too.

So he counted out his money and decided that at last he had enough to satisfy the greedy asking price of the farmer. Ivor walked proudly out of the farmer's house grinning from ear to ear. "The field is ours" he said and Fancy cried all the more! He hugged her, wiped away her tears and took her to the field. He gave her the spade and told her where to dig. She was too tired and sad to argue so she dug and dug. Before she knew it the treasure was in front of them both glinting in the setting sun.

Acetate 5

Her eyes popped out on stalks and she asked Ivor why he hadn't told her. He explained patiently that if anyone had had a hint of what had happened then they risked losing it all. She kissed him and said she forgave him.

Application

Jesus told a story like this. Afterwards, He said that there is a treasure that hardly anyone finds. It is hidden and you cannot see it, but it is still there. Heaven is real, forgiveness is real. The Lord Jesus who died on the cross and rose again form the dead is real. Our sin is real.

Because we live only one life we must find the treasure before it is too late. Ivor knew that he had found something more precious and valuable than anything he had ever known. He lost everything to get it. You see Ivor was just going about his daily business when he found the treasure. It was like he stumbled across it by accident. A friend may have invited you today and you have heard about Jesus perhaps for the first time. He is the greatest treasure of all, "The pearl of great price" We can't see Him with our eyes at the moment because He is in Heaven but He is real. The Bible tells us that Jesus has many names beautiful names which tell us what He is like - The Rose of Sharon, The Light of the World, The Good Shepherd, The Fairest of Ten Thousand, Wonderful, Mighty God.... Jesus is the true treasure - the Bible tells us that in Him "are hidden all the treasures of the wisdom and knowledge" *Colossians 2 v 3*. We must read our Bibles to find out more about Jesus.

There was once a wicked man who stumbled across the true treasure while he was on a journey to throw Christians into prison. His name was Saul and he was travelling to Damascus. He met Jesus on that road and was changed for ever and was forgiven for ever.

If we come to Jesus and ask His forgiveness and ask him to save us from our sins, do you know what He does? The Bible tells us that He makes us his treasured possession - we become like treasure to him - we become beautiful in his sight. We become part of His collection of sparkling jewels. He saves us and changes us. If we are already Christians we may be diamonds in the dust, our brilliance perhaps dimmed by the dust of sin, but one day we shall shake off forever the dust of this earthly life and go to be with Jesus and shine forever with His reflected glory.

What about you? What is the greatest treasure in the world to you? Many people only live for money and getting things like Mr Loadsamoney and they are never satisfied with what they've got - there's always more money to get. One day our life will end and all our money will go to someone else. Will we have found the real treasure by then? Will we have found Jesus?

1   Ivor and Fancy

2 Mr Loadsamoney

3   Ivor and the treasure

4   Fancy and the house

5　　Ivor and Fancy

NOTE TO OHP USERS:

If you have difficulty in getting acetates made of the illustrations used in this book, please contact Moorley's, who can provide a competitive acetate copying service using the original graphics.

Details and prices on application.

MOORLEY'S Print & Publishing

23 Park Rd., Ilkeston, Derbys DE7 5DA
Tel/Fax: (0115) 932 0643

MOORLEY'S are growing Publishers, adding several new titles to our list each year. We also undertake private publications and commissioned works.

Our range of publications
includes: **Books of Verse**
　　　　　Devotional Poetry
　　　　　Recitations
　　　　Drama
　　　　　Bible Plays
　　　　　Sketches
　　　　　Nativity Plays
　　　　　Passiontide Plays
　　　　　Easter Plays
　　　　　Demonstrations
　　　　Resource Books
　　　　　Assembly Material
　　　　　Songs & Musicals
　　　　　Children's Addresses
　　　　　Prayers & Graces
　　　　　Daily Readings
　　　　　Books for Speakers
　　　　Activity Books
　　　　　Quizzes
　　　　　Puzzles
　　　　　Painting Books
　　　　Daily Readings
　　　　Church Stationery
　　　　　Notice Books
　　　　　Cradle Rolls
　　　　　Hymn Board Numbers

Please send a S.A.E. (approx 9" x 6") for the current catalogue or consult your local Christian Bookshop who should stock or be able to order our titles.